D1304299

Just Another Day At Your Local Public Library: An Insider's Tales Of Library Life

Roz Warren

Copyright (c) 2017 Roz Warren

Cover Cartoon © Roz Warren
Cover Design by Dwayne Booth
Cover photo by Carolyn Halper

My Doctor Who T-shirt Is Bigger On The Inside, A Quiet Revolution, and *Reading For Prizes* first appeared on www.broadstreetreview.com.
Bad Librarian!, Librarians! Here's a Little Snark To Lighten Your Day, and *Library Work? It's A Dream* first appeared on www.humoroutcasts.com.
Putting The Cuss In Customer Service first appeared on www.fourthandsycamore.com.
The Inside Poop On Librarian's Daily Adventures first appeared in The Philadelphia Inquirer.
Leaping Librarian! first appeared on www.seniorplanet.com.
Baby Names, Teeth, Chastity and LSD, Is It Ever Okay To Write In A Library Book?, Just Another Day At Your Local Public Library, Library Lost and Found, The Library Witch, Not Sure If You're having Sex? and *Would You Ask A Librarian For A Lap Dance?* first appeared on www.womensvoicesforchange.org.
Are You A Mystery? Or A Trashy Romance?, Checking Out Love At The Library, The Dog Ate My Library Book, Don't Call Me Baby!, How To Make A Librarian Happy, How Quiet Does a Library Have To Be?, I'll Read What She's Reading, It's A Taxing Time To Be A Librarian, The Joy Of Shushing, When Good Things Happen To Bad Library Patrons, and *There's a Banana in the Book Drop!* first appeared on www.zestnow.com.

Published 2017 by HumorOutcasts Press
Printed in the United States of America

ISBN: 0-9980899-5-8
EAN-13: 978-0-9980899-5-9

Also by Roz Warren

Our Bodies, Our Shelves: A Collection of Library Humor

Women's Glib: A Collection of Women's Humor

Men are from Detroit, Women are from Paris: Cartoons By Women About Men

The Best Contemporary Women's Humor

When Cats Talk Back: Cat Cartoons By Women

Women's Glibber: State-Of-The-Art Women's Humor

Women's Lip: Outrageous, Irreverent and Just Plain Hilarious Quotes

Eat, Drink and Remarry; What Women Really Think About Divorce

What Is This Thing Called Sex?

Mothers! Cartoons By Women

Dyke Strippers: Lesbian Cartoonists from A to Z

Revolutionary Laughter: The World of Women Comics

Dedication: To my brilliant, amusing and insightful muses in the ALA Think Tank

and

to Mom, who will always be my favorite librarian. I miss you every day.

Contents

Introduction

Years ago I left the practice of law to take a job at my local public library because I realized that having a lot of fun was more important to me than having a lot of money.

It was the right choice.

I *have* had a lot of fun. Even more important, I've found my tribe. My fellow librarians and library workers are good-hearted, clever, fun-loving, wise and often laugh-out-loud funny. I couldn't have more respect for library folk. They are the absolute best.

I wanted to share the joy of library work, so I began writing about my job for papers like *The Philadelphia Inquirer*, *The Chestnut Hill Local* and *The Christian Science Monitor*, and for websites like Newsworks, Zestnow, The Huffington Post, and Womens Voices For Change.

Because I'm a humorist, I tried to make the essays fun and engaging. But I also felt the need to give the library-going public an honest look at what goes on behind the scenes at a busy public library. Yes, it's a joy to work here. But it isn't always easy. (And while a few readers have chided me for "airing the library's dirty laundry," I believe that knowing about the many challenges we face as we try to provide the public with the best possible service makes our patrons appreciate us even more.)

I'm grateful that my essays about library life have been popular, both with my co-workers and with the public. Nothing makes me happier than when a patron comes into my library and greets me with, "I loved your latest essay!" (Or even, "I read your latest essay and I think you're nuts.")

Two years ago, I published *Our Bodies, Our Shelves*, a collection of twenty humorous library-related essays. Happily, it was well received. *Just Another Day At Your Local Public Library* is my second "library book."

Much of the work in this new collection is crowdsourced. I'll log into one of my favorite online librarian hangouts and ask a question, like "What's the weirdest thing a patron has accused you of doing?" "What's the most outlandish excuse you've ever been given for returning a book late?" Or "How do you really feel about shushing people?"

I'll shape the resulting responses into a piece that explores that topic in a way that is as entertaining (and illuminating) as possible, including as many of the diverse (and often surprising) viewpoints of my fellow librarians and library workers as I can.

This collaboration has been quite a learning experience. My peers have challenged more than one of my own assumptions and I've changed my mind on several issues, like censorship, and just how quiet a library ought to be.

This book also includes a number of essays that voice nobody's opinion but my own, on topics both serious (reparations) and frivolous (the joy of wearing a *Doctor Who* T-shirt to work.)

I've worked at the Bala Cynwyd Library for nearly two decades and I've never once regretted my career switch. I love my job, and I love writing about my job. I'm one of those lucky people who looks forward to going to work every day. And, as a writer and humorist, I'm lucky that the job I love is also a never-ending source of good material.

I hope you enjoy reading this book. I welcome your feedback. Writing is a solitary task and I love hearing from readers. You can praise me, argue with me, share a funny story, suggest an essay topic, book me to speak at your next function and/or send me cute photos of your dog at roswarren@gmail.com.

Roz Warren

Bala Cynwyd, PA

Just Another Day At Your Local Public Library

We librarians are expected to check out your books and answer your reference questions, but we're often called upon to do a wide variety of other things. I recently logged onto Facebook and asked my fellow librarians, "what's the most memorable 'other duty' you've performed since you began your career?"

If you think library work is quiet and humdrum, their responses may surprise you:

"Putting pajamas on a llama. (He was part of a Story Time presentation.)"

"Breaking up fights between moms in our play area."

"Shutting down a couple making whoopee in the

bathroom. (I was the very definition of *coitus interruptus*.)"

"Furnace repair."

"Guiding the bomb squad as they methodically combed through the library for explosives. (Empty phone threat -- phew!)"

"Administering first aid to a patron who'd just been stabbed."

"I do Potty Story Time, so once every three months I spend thirty minutes extolling the virtues of pooping in a toilet to a room full of strangers."

"Posing for stock photos."

"Pulling weeds."

"Shoveling sidewalks."

"Tending chickens."

"Distracting the college student who was hiding out in our library after threatening to shoot his professor until the police could get there and take him into custody."

"Checking to see if the dude who'd been in his car

in our parking lot for hours, motionless, was dead. (He wasn't. Just sound asleep.)"

"Holding a bag containing a baby wallaby so it would stay calm during a Story Time presentation."

"Chasing down and tackling the jerk who grabbed our 'Donate Your Spare Change To The Library' canister and ran out the door with it."

"Removing a black widow spider."

"Helping patrons apply for Moose Permits."

"Climbing onto the roof to retrieve a young patron's favorite stuffed animal."

"Administering CPR to a patron who'd had a coronary in the Reading Room. (He survived.)"

"Making a sign for one of our bathrooms that read: 'There is a live duck in the bathroom. Do not let it out. Use the other bathroom.'"

The next time the line backs up at your library's circulation desk because there's only one librarian on duty instead of the usual two? Don't get angry. That other librarian may be busy fixing the furnace, holding a wallaby, shoveling the sidewalk... or saving a life.

Bad Librarian!

I work at the circulation desk at my local public library. I recently handed a patron's library card back to her after scanning it, but I lost my grip and basically ended up throwing it at her instead. "I'm so sorry!" I said. "I didn't mean to do that."

"Yes you did!" she said.

At first I thought she was joking, but she was dead serious. She really believed that I'd deliberately thrown the card at her. She went ballistic on me, then promised to write an angry letter to my boss and stormed out.

Flabbergasted and shaken, I logged onto Facebook and asked my fellow librarians, "What's the weirdest thing a patron has accused you of doing?"

I got some great responses:

"One patron accused me of being 'out to get her' when I said she couldn't use the computer because she had outstanding library fines. She angrily insisted that we 'go outside and settle this.'"

"A patron once accused me of trying to kill him telepathically because I was Catholic."

"I recently had a patron tell me that my face was wrong for working with children."

"I am often accused of breaking the internet."

"I had a patron repeatedly accuse me of being 'spiritually abusive.' I still haven't figured that one out."

"One of our patrons believes that I am 'stealing her information and sending it to Vladimer Putin.'"

"I've had several patrons accuse me of hiding tax forms."

"I was once accused of being in the Portuguese Mob. (I didn't even know the Portuguese had a mob.)"

"I have been accused of being part of the Seth Myers Clan of the Sea Pirate Mafia. I wish I were joking."

"I was recently accused of being anti-semetic. (I'm Jewish.)"

"I was accused of being a racist because I wouldn't let a woman check out materials without her library card or any identification."

"I've been accused of engaging in cyber espionage and electromagnetic warfare. We've got some serious conspiracy theorists here."

"I've been accused of reading someone's thoughts and then stealing them."

"I had a little girl tell me that I wasn't real because I had the same name as her imaginary friend and her mother had told her that imaginary friends weren't real."

"One of our patrons is convinced that I'm a CIA operative who is stalking her."

"After I asked a member of the cleaning staff to stop leaving her dentures sitting on my desk, she 'rebuked the Satan out of me.'"

"A patron once threatened to kill me when I told him that he had to move his cell phone call out to the lobby."

"A patron who believes that the government is run by Satanic Reptilian Vampires accused me of treason because I refused to help her overthrow them."

"Yesterday a homeless man accused me of moving the toilet when I asked him to stop urinating on the floor."

"I've been told that my whole staff has racist body language."

I was accused of 'making children turn gay' because we have LGBT-supportive books in our junior room collection."

"A woman demanded that I apologize to her son because my aura was so strong that it upset him."

"A white woman who was making a ton of noise accused me, another white woman, of being racist when I asked her to quiet down."

"We have a patron who has accused me of adding fines to his card because I 'have it in for him.'"

"A patron whose internet I blocked lodged a formal complaint against me for interfering with his 'basic human right to watch pornography.'"

"A patron once submitted a written formal complaint about me for 'smiling too much.' He said it wasn't professional."

It may be unprofessional for a librarian to smile, but by the time I was done reading these comments, I had a big grin on my face. The lesson? You just can't let the hotheads and the crazies get you down. Instead, you have to laugh. The important thing is that I wasn't alone. My fellow librarians had my back.

And just like that, I was back to loving my job.

But the next time I'm wrongly accused by a paranoid patron? I just might enlist my pals in the Seth Myers Clan of the Sea Pirates Mafia to steal her information and send it to Vladimir Putin.

The Dog Ate My Library Book

The art of storytelling is alive and well, which is something you soon learn when you work at a public library. I'm not talking about the stories in the books. I'm talking about the amazing excuses patrons dream up to weasel out of paying library fines. Although most library patrons are honest, upstanding people, some folks will say anything to get out of paying the money they owe us. I recently asked my fellow librarians to share the most memorable fine avoidance lines their patrons have handed them over the years.

Here are a few of the best:

"The books were lost in a landslide. It was an act of nature so I shouldn't have to pay."

"The TSA confiscated my DVDs."

"I threw them all away because another librarian told me that was okay."

"I've been way too busy to renew my books."

"When a bee flew in my car, I panicked and grabbed the book and threw it at the bee and the book went out the window. On the freeway. So I couldn't stop."

"A literary thug broke into my car and took them all."

"Return them? I had no idea that I had to return them!"

"I loaned them to my therapist and she didn't give them back. This is really giving me trust issues."

"I was in the middle of writing my thesis when my boyfriend broke up with me, stole all my library books and deleted my research."

"These are Christian books! You can't fine people for reading Christian books!"

"They were destroyed in a prison riot."

"I really hated the book, so I shouldn't have to pay for bringing it back late."

"My poodle chewed it up and then barfed all over a priceless Oriental rug. I should be charging *you*."

"It was a book about witchcraft and it was burned, but I shouldn't be charged for it because Satan set it on fire."

"I lost it in a tornado."

"My twin stole my driver's license, got a library card in my name, checked out a bunch of stuff, then skipped town."

"I couldn't return the books on time because I was undergoing surgery. What kind of surgery? Breast augmentation! Does that matter?"

"My exterminator took them."

"The book came back water-damaged because I got caught in a downpour. That's an act of God, right? So I shouldn't have to pay."

"I checked those books out so that they wouldn't be a danger to kids and I refuse to pay the fines because I'm doing the community a service by keeping the Devil at bay."

"I gave birth to my baby on the side of the interstate

and the books were ruined by the … fluid." (Library staff actually Googled this news story. She was telling the truth! Her overdue fines were waived but she did have to pay to replace the books.)

If you're the kind of library patron who hands us a line instead of paying your fine, why not put pen to paper and channel all the creative energy you're using to lie to us into something more productive? Maybe you can write a best seller! Then you'd easily be able to afford to pay the money you owe us.

Until then, we librarians will continue to roll our eyes when you roll out your latest lame excuse.

My Doctor Who T-shirt Is Bigger On The Inside

When I saw the *Doctor Who* T-shirt on display at my favorite comic book store I knew I had to have it. This might sound more like something a teenage Fan Girl would say than a 60-year-old librarian. But I've always been a little quirky, and, like many librarians, I'm a serious *Doctor Who* fan.

Doctor Who is a BBC TV show that first went on the air in 1963 and holds the world record for the longest-running televised science-fiction series, with 827 episodes so far.

The show's protagonist, "the Doctor," is a Time Lord who travels through time and space, saving the universe and having adventures. Why do I love the show? It's just like library work!

No, I'm kidding. It's about as far from library work

as you can get, which is probably why it's so much fun. After an afternoon spent searching for missing books and wrangling with patrons about paying overdue fines, it's a pleasant relief to watch somebody else battling alien monsters and saving the universe.

The T-shirt I coveted pictured the cover of Abbey Road, but instead of John, Paul, George and Ringo crossing the street, it's four popular *Doctor Who* villains -- a Dalek, a Cyberman, a Silent and a Weeping Angel.

"I love it!" I said to the store clerk. "But I haven't worn a fan shirt like that in years."

"Why not try it on?" she suggested.

It fit me perfectly.

I left the practice of law years ago to take a job at my local public library. There were many good reasons for this choice, one of which was the dress code. I happily went from power suits and heels to casual clothes and comfy shoes.

You can't work at a law firm wearing a *Dr. Who* T-shirt. But at a public library? No problem.

As a teenager in the 70s, I often wore T-shirts celebrating things that were close to my heart. "Stop The War." "Frodo Lives." "A Woman Without A Man Is Like A Fish Without A Bicycle." But when I grew up, went to law school and began practicing law, I got out of the T-shirt habit.

It was time, I decided, to jump back in.

The first time I came to work wearing my new *Doctor Who* T-shirt, I gained instant approval from our teenage pages. "Great shirt!" several of them told me.

As for the patrons? Most didn't notice. A few asked me to explain my shirt. But my fellow Whovians? We bonded instantly and began talking *Who*. "Who's your favorite doctor?" "How do you feel about River Song?" "Don't you just love it when they reverse the polarity?"

Once I realized how much fun it was to wear T-shirts to work, I dug some of my old favorites out of the closet and wore them too. And I've begun to acquire new ones.

I've even discovered T-shirts about library work. "Choose Books." "Reading Is My Superpower."

"What Happens In The Library Stays In The Library." But the *Doctor Who* shirt that triggered my T-shirt renaissance is still my favorite. I wear it so often that it's like a second skin. I'll forget that I have it on until I pass a kid on the street who calls out "Cool shirt!"

Wearing a cool T-shirt also gives folks an easy way to connect with me. One look and you've got a good excuse to start a conversation.

"But you're 60- years-old! A librarian!" you might protest. "Where's your sense of dignity?"

When I abandoned lawyering for library work, I chose fun over dignity. I embraced a work world that enables me to do things like dance around like a goofball singing to babies and toddlers at Story Time rather than striding, suit-clad, into court.

Whenever I put on my *Doctor Who* T-shirt, I make that choice all over again.

Would You Ask A Librarian For A Lap Dance?

In the many years that I've worked at my local public library, I've learned that we librarians do plenty of things for our patrons that aren't in our job descriptions. After a patron asked me to change her flat tire, and another pleaded with me to let her check out our pencil sharpener, I logged onto Facebook and asked my fellow librarians, "What's the oddest thing a patron has ever asked you to do?"

The first response?

"Someone just asked me for a good book to read on the toilet."

Quickly followed by:

"A patron who was on his way to the casino asked if he could rub my red hair for good luck."

23

"Last week a woman came in who said she needed my help to get the witches and demons to stop pinching her."

"A patron once asked me to sit on his lap. (I laughed at him.)"

Unusual patron requests proved to be a hot topic. Within a day, I had over a hundred responses, as librarians shared stories about that special patron who:

"… asked if she could leave her kids at the circ desk with me while she ran errands."

"…wanted me to find books to prove that he was Julius Caesar, reincarnated."

"… asked me to tell the man sitting at the computer next to hers to stop controlling her computer with his thoughts."

"…brought in a mounted wildebeest head and asked if we could store it in the archives for the summer."

It became clear that Odd Patron Requests fell into categories. For instance? Patrons who wanted to look their best, with our help.

"A woman once asked if she could trade pants with me because she was going on a job interview."

"A man once asked me to use library tape to remove lint from his suit jacket."

"One man asked if he could use our community meeting room to shave with an electric razor. ('Is the power out at your house?' I asked. 'Nope,' he said. No further explanation.)"

"After asking me a reference question, one patron pulled a toothbrush from her fanny pack and went to town on her teeth as I spoke. And when that was done, she brought out the dental floss."

Some requests were automotive:

"People have been known to come to the reference desk and ask if we have jumper cables."

"A patron once asked to borrow my car."

"One of our regulars asked me to drive her to a town two hours away so she could look at apartments."

There were numerous requests for library hanky panky:

"Last week, a patron asked me to have sex with him in the alley. I didn't."

"A 60-year-old guy asked the head of our Junior Room to join him in the rest room. No dice."

"One patron asked me to meet him in the copy room. (Wink wink.) Sorry, no."

"I once had a male patron in his 50s who wouldn't leave the reference desk until I told him he was naughty. (Handled by stating, deadpan, no eye contact, 'Go on with your bad self, then.')"

Librarians have been asked to break the law:

"A patron once offered me $100 to go into somebody's yard and steal a cactus."

"I've been offered $50 to help a patron create a fake passport."

"One patron wanted me to tell her my son's social security number so she could use it to get more financial assistance. (I said no.)"

Many unusual library questions are medical in nature:

"One patron appeared in my office doorway holding a cotton swab and a petri dish and began by saying, 'You can totally say no to this....' (I did.)"

"Let's just say that if I wanted to diagnose athlete's foot, I'd have a MD, not a MLIS."

Some patrons want to take our innate helpfulness and eagerness to serve the public to the next level:

"One patron phoned to ask if I could check out a list of books for her and drop them off at her house."

"A patron once asked for my home phone number so she could phone me with reference questions when I wasn't at work. Patrons have also asked me to do their taxes, clean their homes, and perform at their children's birthday parties."

"A patron recently asked if he could borrow $7,000."

"A woman once asked me to go look for a dead body she was sure was buried by a lake, because the police wouldn't listen to her."

We are also called upon to identify things:

"A patron once asked me to identify a dead bug

she'd taped to a piece of notebook paper."

"I was asked to identify the snake a patron had caught (and brought into the library) in a bucket."

One patron approached the reference desk with 'There's a brownish-grey fluffy animal under my porch. What is it?'"

We've also been called upon to research a variety of interesting topics:

"One patron wanted me to find a book she could use to teach her dog German."

"I've been asked to research how to avoid being cloned without your permission."

"A patron once asked me to direct her to the books about Brazil written specifically for unborn children."

"I once received a reference query from an inmate at a local correctional facility for books on how to levitate."

Librarians are helpful by nature, which means that often we have no problem going above and beyond our job descriptions to perform small acts of library kindness:

"An elderly woman just asked me to tie her shoes for her. (I did. She was too old to bend down and reach them herself.)"

"A patron recently asked me to help her find the tune and lyrics to patriotic songs so she could sing them to her Marine boyfriend on their upcoming road trip to the state capital. (Sadly, this woman has a mental illness, and there was no boyfriend or road trip, but I treated the question as if there were.)"

Despite the odd requests, we librarians remain undaunted. We continue to love library work. And, of course, everyone loves a library story with a happy ending? For instance? My own favorite response to the question I posed about unusual requests, which was:

"A divorced dad came to Story Hour, asked me out, then (after we'd dated for a few months) asked me to marry him!! I did!"

The Inside Poop On Librarians' Daily Adventures

A man recently took a dump in the stairwell at the Ludington Library in Bryn Mawr, Pennsylvania. The deed and the defecator's subsequent exit from the building were both captured by the library's security cameras, and the local police circulated footage of the *perp* leaving the library and asked the public to help identify him. (What did he look like? An ordinary, somewhat distracted-looking middle-aged guy. If you passed him on the street you wouldn't look at him twice.)

It's safe to say that the library-going public was shocked and horrified by what he did. It's also safe to say that nobody who has ever worked at a public library was in the least bit surprised.

What this man did is a fact of library life, which was reflected in the online comments of librarians all over the country when the story was reported in the press:

"The public has no idea how often this happens."

"Happened to me just last week. My first week as a branch manager. What a welcome."

"Everyone who visits our library comments on our beautifully patterned carpet squares. If only they knew *why* we chose those easily removable squares!"

"Two summers ago we had a guy who left daily 'presents' all over the building. We never knew where they'd turn up next. Worst game of *Where's Waldo* EVER."

Everyone is welcome at your local public library. But not everyone does (or can) behave as well as we'd like. Both our very youngest and our very oldest patrons will, inevitably, have "accidents." And then there are the troubled or angry individuals who do this stuff on purpose.

The sad reality is that no place in a public library is immune. Librarians tell of finding "deposits" in the stacks. Under a table in the quiet study room. By the internet computers. On a comfy chair in the reading nook. In the book drop. Once, mysteriously, right in front of the reference desk on a day when the library was packed.

And do certain patrons occasionally play Jackson Pollack on our bathroom walls with their own waste? Alas, yes.

The Ludington Pooper, most assumed, was a troubled individual. Which, when he was identified (Thanks, internet!) turned out to be the case. Let's hope he'll get the help he so clearly needs.

Librarians everywhere were happy that he'd been captured on camera, and could be apprehended and stopped. But we all know that this kind of activity remains an ongoing challenge.

My hope is that this incident won't be (so to speak) a total waste. Perhaps it will raise the public's consciousness about what being a librarian is actually like. I love my job, but it isn't always easy.

People imagine that librarians spend our days in a serene, untroubled environment, working with books and chatting with patrons.

"You're so lucky," I've been told. "You get paid to read!"

We do read. Sometimes. We also endure your wrath about paying fines, move heaven and earth to find the book you need, spread tarp over the shelves when the ceiling leaks, recommend a movie that will fascinate your daughter's preteen pals at her sleepover party without offending any of their mothers, attempt to stop you from tearing pages out of our magazines, knock ourselves out to entertain your kids at Story Time, teach you how to open your own email, listen with sympathy to your confidences and -- unfortunately -- occasionally have to clean up after you.

You're welcome.

Is It Ever Okay To Write In A Library Book?

When I first started working at my local public library I was surprised to learn that there are library patrons who actually correct -- in ink -- the spelling and grammatical errors they find in our books. At first, I thought this was a good thing. The way I saw it, these unsung heroes, by maintaining standards of literacy in an age of creeping Twitter-speak, were performing a valuable public service.

I began to re-think this when it came to my attention that we also have patrons who have taken it upon themselves to edit out, with a felt-tipped pen, any cursing, profanity or sexually explicit behavior they encounter in the material they've checked out.

I am now, like most librarians, an absolutist when it comes to defacing library property. You can do whatever you like to your personal copy of a book. Annotate it! Highlight it! Cross out the parts you don't like! Rip it apart and use it for collage!

But leave our books alone.

And yet, there are librarians who deface library books themselves. A recent post on my favorite library-related Facebook page described an elementary school librarian who drew boxer briefs on the naked little boy in Maurice Sendak's classic children's book *In The Night Kitchen*. Because her school serves a conservative neighborhood, she was worried that parents might be upset if a child brought the book home.

Their responses to this post made it clear that my fellow librarians were not down with this:

"That's censorship, plain and simple. And it's wrong."

"Prudes have been defacing this book since it first came out in 1970. I really thought we'd gotten past this by now."

"If Maurice Sendak had wanted the kid to be wearing boxers, he'd have drawn them on himself. Nobody has any business bowdlerizing someone else's work."

"She's defacing a work of art. If it's not okay to paint clothing on a nude at a museum, why is it okay to do this?"

"As a parent, I'd be extremely disappointed to find that a library book had been defaced like this."

"This is not only unacceptable and ridiculous, it's a gross ethical violation. Somebody please stop her."

And yet, other comments made it clear that librarians defacing library property is nothing new:

"I once worked with a school library technician who took it upon herself to draw shirts on all the bare-chested people in *National Geographic*."

"I'm a school librarian. My predecessor had a cache of 'banned books' hidden away in a locked cabinet, including a book that contained a photo of a woman breast-feeding. When I took over, I re-shelved them all."

We considered the question of whether librarians are there to enforce community standards:

"In her defense, the FCC demands that certain

words be 'bleeped' before a show can air. So you could argue that there's a precedent for community standards being applied."

"But she defaced the book before anyone complained! It wasn't done in response to community concern."

"Censorship is a slippery slope. What else offends (or scares) this librarian? And who put her in charge of community morals?"

"They do this kind of thing to newspapers in Saudi Arabia. Not a good model to imitate."

The clear consensus? Good librarians don't deface or censor books:

"If somebody did this in my library, I'd buy a new copy and discard the damaged one."

"I'm a school librarian at a Catholic school. We have *In The Night Kitchen*, uncensored, in our collection. We also have science books about the human body that have scientific drawings (at a kid's level) of labia and penises. Kids need to learn about sexual anatomy. It's 'private,' yes, but it's nothing to be ashamed of."

"I've had parents complain about this book. It's still on our shelves. Don't like it? Don't read it."

My favorite response? The librarian who cited Kurt Cobain:

"When asked to alter the cover art of Nirvana's *Nevermind*, which showed a naked three-year-old (with penis clearly visible) swimming toward a dollar bill, lead singer Cobain agreed to only one compromise -- a strategically placed sticker that would read: 'If you're offended by this, you must be a closet pedophile.' The original album art went out untouched."

While I'm happy to replace the stereotype of the uptight cardigan-wearing librarian with that of an edgy, Cobain-quoting librarian, the final word has to go to New Jersey librarian Cynthia Robbins:

"I read this book over and over again to my daughter without any bad result. It was her favorite. Adults pass on their own bad feelings when they censor like this. Censorship is fear. As librarians, we are supposed to be fearless."

I agree. Although I am, by nature, quiet and mild-mannered, I want to be fearless when it comes to standing up for the books in our collection. And let's face it -- if you're a librarian who can't deal with defending Maurice Sendak's right to draw a little boy without his clothes on, you're probably in the wrong profession.

And if you're a parent who doesn't want her kid to see a fictional five-year old's penis? You can buy yourself a copy of *In The Night Kitchen* and deface it to your heart's content.

Of course, if your kid ever checks the book out of the school library, he's in for a surprise.

Library Work? It's A Dream

I recently had a dream in which one of our most challenging patrons apologized for always being a nuisance, then meekly paid all her fines. This was so startling that I immediately woke up. Inspired, I went online and asked my fellow librarians, "Do you ever dream about library work?"

It turns out that I'm not the only librarian who dreams about her job:

"I dreamed about cataloging biographies last night."

"I dream about shelving books all the time. I've been told by my husband that I make shelving motions in my sleep."

"I had a dream that we were trying to close for the day but the patrons refused to leave. We were

41

turning off the computers and they were turning them back on again."

"My recurring nightmare: due to funding cuts, *all* of the library's lighting has been removed, making it very difficult to shelve books."

"I often dream that I'm working in a library that I don't know with people I *do* know."

"I dreamt that my library hired Jimmy Fallon to work as a reference librarian. (We all really liked him but he wouldn't answer reference questions. He just told jokes. We didn't know what to do about him.)"

"I recently dreamt that I opened a closet and was buried in catalog cards. Easy to figure that one out."

"I often dream about work… and I frequently solve actual work problems in my dreams."

"I dream that I'm shelving books and the Dewey Decimal numbers rearrange themselves just to mock me."

"One of my co-workers had a dream in which he couldn't find the Reserves shelf because I'd shifted it and wouldn't tell him where it was."

"I dreamed that somebody had mixed all the 641s and 746s together and I had just thirty minutes to fix it. Of course, *Final Jeopardy* music was playing and several people with clipboards were watching…."

"I have a recurring dream in which I get up in front of my Story Time crowd and realize that I'm completely unprepared, the moms tell me that I'm the worst librarian ever and all the kids start to cry."

"Last night I dreamt that I was working with a student who was researching Russian media. (I found her some terrific resources, and was disappointed, when I woke up, that she wasn't real.)"

"I often dream about finding supply closets I'd never seen before and getting mad at my co-workers for not telling me about them."

"A while back our library had a lot of books that needed shifting. I dreamt that I was doing it all night. And when I got to work the next day I had to do it all over again."

"I have this dream all the time: We're trying to lock the doors at closing but people just stream in through the unlocked ones."

"I had a dream that for some reason one of our Library Board members was forbidden to come into the library. I was working the desk and looked up to see one of my co-workers wrestling with him in the entranceway."

"I had a dream that somebody was moving all the books on the shelves around and I couldn't tell them not to. All I could do was sit there and watch the destruction."

"I dreamed that our digital media lab instructor challenged me to a *West Side Story* style gang rumble, so I grew Wolverine claws and shredded his leather jacket. He conceded defeat. (I work with this guy all the time and we get along great so I don't know where that came from.)"

"I just had a dream that my house was attached to the library, and my kids opened the doors too early. I was running around the library in my pajamas trying to get everything ready when it dawned on me that my pajamas violated the dress code! So I ran back to my house to change and found one of my most problematic patrons rifling through my closet. Then I woke up. But that panicky feeling stuck with me all day."

"I had a dream that the TARDIS was broken and I was trying to work with the Doctor to fix it, but I kept getting interrupted by library patrons."

"Neil Gaiman once came to the reference desk in my dream and we chatted about books. I was sad to wake up."

"I had a dream about a young teen who asked for books with the word 'blue' in the title. She said that's all she would read. I thought of half a dozen actual Young Adult books with 'blue' in the title. (And they were real books, too, not just weird dream titles.) She was pleased and I woke up feeling accomplished."

What -- if anything -- do these library dreams mean? Who knows? Of course, I can look it up. The Dewey Decimal number for books about Dreams is 135.

Or perhaps I'll just go to sleep tonight and dream about doing it.

There's A Banana In The Book Drop!

Life holds plenty of surprises, especially when you work at a public library. Last week, for instance, we found a banana in the book drop. Naturally, I logged onto Facebook to share the news:

The first response?

"Curious George strikes again!"

Then:

"We once found a melted banana split in ours."

After which my fellow librarians began listing the items they'd found over the years in their own book drops:

"A full diaper."

"A dead rabbit."

"An empty wine bottle."

"A used condom."

"We found underpants in ours yesterday. But they were clean!"

A banana was beginning to seem like a relatively delightful book find. Reports of more discoveries poured in:

"A slice of bacon."

"A cell phone."

"A live lobster."

"A laptop."

"An ice cream sandwich. Thankfully it was winter, so it hadn't melted."

"A coffee maker. People be crazy."

As more responses came in, I began to wonder. Was there anything that *hadn't* been left in a library book drop?

"A dead fish."

"A live chicken!"

"A small tub of cottage cheese."

"A cat."

"A bra."

"A dirty love letter! (And yes, we all read it.)"

"In my own workplace, a lit joint in the book drop is not unheard of."

As librarians warmed to the topic, book drop discoveries came in fast and furious:

"A frog!"

"Pancake syrup."

"A lizard."

"An unopened box of sanitary pads."

"A full bottle of Jim Beam.

"A bag of grapes."

"A carton of eggs."

"One of my co-workers used to get gifts in the book drop from a secret admirer."

Think that working in a library is all sunshine and roses? Contemplate these book drop finds and think again:

"A dead bird in a shoe box with a note threatening the life of our library mascot, a cockatiel."

"Seventeen snakes."

"A finger. Yes, an actual finger. We never found out whose. And it was my first week on the job."

Library patrons can be mysterious:

"We once found a wrapped Subway sandwich in the book drop. Later that week, we found another one on the shelves. Weird."

"Nothing odd in our book drop yet. But someone once put a hot dog in our suggestion box."

"Somebody just left a deer head on our roof."

"Last week somebody removed a garden gnome from a nearby house and put it in our book drop."

Some folks just don't deserve a book drop:

"My library got rid of our book drop the second time it was set on fire."

"Some idiot poured gasoline in ours. Now we have security cameras."

"Our book drop was destroyed. We don't know who did it, but we came to work one morning to find that somebody had beat the living hell out of it."

Finally? Librarians would like to remind you that real patriots don't include the library book drop in their celebration of our nation's birth:

"If we don't close our drop over the fourth of July weekend, people put firecrackers in it."

Library life is full of discovery. And when it comes to the book drop, it seems, anything is possible! Which is why I'm hoping that the next time I open ours, I'll find it packed with hundred dollar bills. Or Oreo cookies. I'd even settle for that lit joint.

A librarian can dream, can't she?

The Joy Of Shushing

I'm a librarian and I enjoy shushing people. Shutting down somebody who is blathering away at top volume on their cell phone in the Quiet Reading Room is one of the joys of library work. Am I alone in this? Apparently not. When I recently posted my I-love-to-shush confession on my favorite Facebook librarian hangout, it earned eighty-two "Likes." As well as forty-three comments, both pro and con. How does your librarian really feel about shushing you? Here's a sampling:

"I never hesitate to shush. Indoor voices, please."

"I never shush. Shushing stresses me out."

"Shushing is appropriate for people hollering on cell phones, but not when people are having an engaging debate or conversation."

"The way one librarian chooses to quiet people has an effect on all librarians, and on our brand. Hopefully we can shush without being mean about it."

"I have no need to shush. As a seasoned librarian, I have 'the look' down."

"I don't shush. Instead, I perform a little gesture with my arms that signals 'Keep it down.' That gesture, with a friendly smile, usually does the trick."

"Sometimes it helps to point out to the loudmouth that everyone around them can hear their conversation."

"I was on my way over to quiet a patron once and before I reached her, she'd managed to broadcast her credit card information to the entire library. One can only hope that the quiet-loving patrons who were using our computers didn't immediately go to their favorite online stores and start charging things to her."

"I was once talking loudly to a patron who is hard of hearing and another patron, with a furious look, shushed *me*. (Was she embarrassed when I explained the situation to her? You bet.)"

"I only shush if I absolutely must. I see it as a necessary evil, but I don't enjoy it."

"I hate to shush. I do it very politely but I've still been sworn at, called a 'Library Nazi,' and worst of all, been totally ignored."

"I *hate* doing it. I only do it when another patron asks me to. I try to be polite but firm, but I'm always worried that I come off as being rude."

"I consider my ability to shush to be one of my superpowers as a librarian. But I use it sparingly."

"Our library is a Shush-Free Zone. We aren't *allowed* to shush people."

"A patron once told *me* to 'lower my voice an octave.' Still scratching my head about that one."

"A woman was talking on her cell yesterday with her speaker on. When I asked her to take it outside she said loudly, 'I gotta go. The librarian just told me to shut up.' That's *not* what I said."

"Sometimes it has to be done, but it always makes

me anxious."

"A woman recently sat down at a table in the quiet reading area, pulled out her laptop and proceeded to participate in a back-and-forth that we could hear from across the room. When I asked her to keep the volume down, she hissed, 'Don't you tell me to be quiet. This is a webinar!'"

"I could really use a nice big 'Quiet' sign."

"I'd prefer a nice big ray gun."

"I usually throw a dictionary at them. Is that wrong? (Wink.)"

"Ideally we could lob a book at any patron who ticked us off. *That* would be a fun library to work in. I'd love to stockpile *The Total Idiot's Guide To Good Manners* behind the circulation desk for just that purpose."

"One of our librarians makes use of a decibel meter app. Our patrons seem to appreciate that approach."

"I never shush. Although I have been known to walk up to a group of loud patrons and say, 'Don't *make* me shush you!'"

"I don't enjoy shushing people. On the other hand, I do appreciate the looks of gratitude I get from other patrons when I quell someone who is being oblivious and obnoxious."

What can we conclude? Library work has changed a lot over the decades, but the library's value as an oasis of peace and quiet has not. Nor has the librarian's time-honored ability to shush. Loud in the library? Many of us, it seems, do not relish the task of shutting you down.   As for me? Go ahead. Make my day.

When Good Things Happen To Bad Library Patrons

If you think that life is fair, just take a job at your local public library.

Although I was raised to believe that playing by the rules is always the right thing to do, library work has certainly undermined that. Over and over, I see people not playing fair, and getting away with it.

For instance? Patrons lie to us constantly.

"I returned that book!"

"I never checked that DVD out!"

"Your computer is wrong. I returned those CDs on time."

"That magazine was covered with food stains and missing a dozen pages when I checked it out!"

And because our policy is to take our patrons at their word unless we have hard evidence to the contrary, they usually get away with it.

Sometimes, they don't. We cherish those moments when, despite a liar's best efforts, the truth comes to light. I once told a patron that the Jennifer Weiner novel she had out on her card was long overdue.

"You're wrong!" she said. "I clearly remember returning it. Take it off my account immediately."

Then her daughter, who'd been quietly standing beside her, spoke up. "You didn't return it, Mom," she said. "I saw it this morning on your nightstand."

Busted!

But for the most part, these moments are few and far between. Instead? To weasel out of paying fines, patrons will sneak an overdue book back onto the shelf, then claim that they returned it weeks ago.

Rather than paying the hundreds of dollars in unpaid fines on their card, they'll open a new card for their kid, and proceed to check out their own books on that card.

Or they'll check out twenty brand new DVDs, then leave town and never return them.

All of this bad behavior goes unpunished. Meanwhile, good patrons follow the rules and pay their fines without fussing.

Enough of this can seriously distort the way you look at your fellow man. When a new co-worker's husband asked about her first week on the job, she told him, "My co-workers are great! But our patrons are all a bunch of bald-faced liars!"

I used to have a friend who didn't believe the rules applied to him. He was the kind of guy who always cut lines. If traffic was backed up, he'd drive in the break-down lane. When I told him how uncomfortable this made me feel, he proclaimed "Following the rules is for chumps!"

After years of library work, I'm in danger of agreeing with him.

"What goes around, comes around," a co-worker who believes in karma once assured me. "If somebody behaves badly, you may think they're getting away with it. But sooner or later? Life will bite them in the butt."

Maybe so. But all I see is people breaking our rules and lying to us again and again, and nobody's butt is getting bitten.

Another co-worker will take the word of any patron, no matter how outrageous or implausible their lie. Why?

"I believe in a higher power," she tells me. "If that patron is lying to me, God will handle it."

I wish I had her faith.

When I first began library work, I found the unfairness of it all very difficult to tolerate. But, to enjoy my job, I've had to learn to live with the fact that selfish people get away with doing bad things and there's nothing I can do about it.

Of course, my co-workers and I all know exactly who these people are and we heartily dislike them for it. We complain about them to each other. We mock them behind their backs. When they approach the circulation desk, we sigh and roll our eyes.

We joke that the next time one of them is checking out a book, we'll hand them a copy of *Ethical*

Behavior for Dummies and say "Perhaps you'd like to take this out too?"

We'd never actually do that, of course. That would be rude. And librarians are never rude.

So. If you're the kind of person who habitually breaks the rules and lies to your librarian, is the fact that she thinks you're a jerk punishment enough?

I'd like to think so. But if I told you that I really believe this? I'd be the one who was lying.

Checking Out Love At The Library

I'm 61 and newly single. How to find Mr. Right? "That's easy!" I'm told. "You work at a library. There's nothing sexier than a bookish man. You'll have your pick of terrific guys!"

The author of a recent article about how to meet potential dates agrees. She passes along this tip: "Go to the public library and cruise the shelves for smart singles."

Is this really good advice? When I logged onto Facebook and asked my fellow librarians, "Is your library a good place to look for love?" the first comment I got wasn't encouraging:

"Let's see. When it comes to our regulars, I can choose from Alcoholic Homeless Guy, Ranting Political Guy or Porn-Viewing Guy. No thanks."

But the next response was more upbeat:

"I definitely recommend looking for love at the library. It's where I met my husband!"

Over the next day, I received dozens of comments expressing a range of opinions.

For many librarians, the answer to the question "Should I look for love at my local public library?" was a resounding, "Hell, no!"

"Yeah, I'd really want to hook up with our Conspiracy Theorist. Or the elusive sicko who poops in our potted plants."

"The Uber-Religious-Witnessing Guy is the big catch at our library!"

"Finding romance? Right. Great idea. Just go up to random people and ask, 'What are you reading?' Because there's nothing I love more than having my reading interrupted to talk to a stranger about it."

"Sadly, my library is a better place to find your next hit than to be hit on."

"In an ideal world, you'd meet fellow intellectuals at the library. In the real world? You're more likely to meet a guy who'll warn you that the Martian spaceships are about to land."

Other librarians felt that library love, if not a sure thing, was at least a possibility:

"I'd never come here looking for love. But if you're at the library and you happen to see someone attractive reading one of your favorite books? That's not a bad conversation starter."

"You could find love here if you attended our lectures and readings. Participating in a program that you're interested in is a good way to meet like-minded people."

"There have been no matches made yet between library staff and patrons, but our single librarians remain hopeful. When a cute guy comes in, we've been known to check his account to see if he's married or available."

Other librarians were totally in favor of finding love at the library:

"Judging by the hetero couples who duck into the men's room together, some folks are definitely finding romance here. (If romance is the right word for it…)"

"I met my husband while working at the front desk. The book he wanted wasn't available, so I bought a paperback copy at a used book store and added it to our collection, then phoned him and told him he could come in and pick it up. He ended up picking me up too, and we've been together twenty-five years."

But? Proceed with caution.

"A young woman recently came to my library to use one of our computers. The minute I saw her, I knew that she'd be hassled by some of our resident Casanovas. Sure enough, within minutes they were circling her like sharks at feeding time. When she asked me for help with the document she was working on, I took the opportunity to ask if any of the guys had been harassing her, to which she replied, 'Yeah, they're all trying to get a piece of this. If they only knew I just got out of jail for stabbing my ex.'"

In conclusion? Although nothing is certain, it's entirely possible to find love at the library. (And if you're a good-hearted, bookish, 60ish guy, let me encourage you to visit mine.)

Even if you don't leave with a date, you'll never

have to leave alone.

You can always take home *The Girl On The Train*, *Madame Bovary, A Man Called Ove* or *Alexander Hamilton*.

Just make sure to be on your best behavior, because while you're checking that book out, the singletons behind the circ desk might be checking *you* out.

Reading For Prizes

If you work in a public library, summer means (cue drum roll and crash of cymbals) ...the Summer Reading Club! The SRC used to be just for kids, to motivate them to read when school wasn't in session. But in recent years many libraries, mine included, have expanded the program to include grown-ups too.

I've never been crazy about the Summer Reading Club. I believe that people ought to read for the sheer pleasure of it, not for prizes. Nevertheless, as a circulation assistant, my job includes trying to enroll as many of our patrons as possible.

"Once you join," I explain, dozens of times a day, "you submit a brief review of each book you read. Every week we have a drawing, and if your review is chosen, you win a prize!"

"What kind of prize?" they'll ask.

"It could be a Ferrari!" I'll joke. "Or a yacht! Or even a trip to Paris! But seriously? It's a gift basket filled with treats, like teas and jams and chocolate."

Our library used to be pretty laid-back about Summer Reading. We'd post a few signs about the club and if a patron asked to join, we'd sign them up. Enrollment was minimal, and that was fine with us.

But this year we have a new boss, and it matters to Carolyn that we sign up lots of people. (Why? Competition with other libraries? Patron involvement? The fact that she's freshly graduated from library school and thus beautifully un-jaded and un-cynical about everything library-related, including Summer Reading?)

Carolyn is a peach, so unlike prior years, when I could safely ignore the whole thing, I now have to take the SRC seriously. Which means? Keeping my true feelings to myself and knocking myself out to get you to join.

In the old days, I only bothered to ask folks I knew

would say yes. If a woman in her fifties brought a stack of mysteries to the circ desk for check out, I'd give her the pitch. But a dude in his twenties who only checks out DVDs? Why bother?

Now, I challenged myself to ask everyone. Cheerfully! Optimistically! With no exceptions. I was through with Patron Profiling. For the greater good of the Bala Cynwyd Library, I would ask each and every person to join, even when I knew there wasn't a chance in hell that they'd say yes.

And guess what? Our patrons surprised me.

A man checks out a stack of CDs, but not a single book. Clearly, not a reader. And yet, when I ask, "Would you like to join our Summer Reading Club?" his eyes light up and I get an enthusiastic "Yes!'

But when I try to recruit a woman who has just placed a slew of bestsellers on hold, certain that she'll agree, I get a firm "No, thanks!"

Clearly, I don't know our patrons as well as I thought I did.

Of course, some of my assumptions do hold true. Women are more likely to join than men, and

Seniors more likely to join than Millennials. Still, far more Millennials and men say yes than I would have expected.

It almost makes me regret ignoring them in the past.

Almost. Because I still, at heart, have little love for the SRC. If nobody joined, that would suit me just fine. And yet, I find myself not only selling the heck out of the thing, but taking pride in how many people I've been able to sign up.

Selling the SRC turns out to be something I'm very good at. In fact, I'm better at convincing people to join than anyone else in the library.

Who knew?

I've signed up dozens. By summer's end, I plan to sign up hundreds! Why? Because it matters to my boss and I'm a team player. Plus, our patrons enjoy participating. They like sharing their opinions about the books they've read. And the possibility of winning a prize.

When we handed the winner of the first drawing her gift basket, she was so thrilled that we could have been handing her the keys to a new Ferrari.

Does this mean I've been wrong about the SRC all along? Call me a book snob, but I still believe that reading should be its own reward. Which doesn't mean that when you come to my library I'm not going to do whatever it takes to get you to join.

My pal, Melissa Schnapp, who is a life coach, is always encouraging me to practice gratitude. "Don't focus on how much you dislike the idea of reading for prizes," she says. "Focus on what you're grateful for."

I am grateful for this job, which I love. And for our wonderful patrons and my terrific new boss. I am grateful that I'm smart enough to figure out how to con, manipulate, persuade, cajole and/or entice people into doing what I want them to do.

And I am very grateful that summer doesn't last forever.

Baby Names, Teeth, Chastity and LSD

Last week a patron at the library where I work spent five minutes telling one of my co-workers all about why (and exactly how) she should use a waterpick. This inspired me to go online and ask my fellow librarians, "What's the oddest thing a library patron has ever said to you?"

Within a day, I had dozens of responses. Here's a sampling:

"A woman just asked me to help name her baby."

"I've been asked how to make LSD."

"Two topics that are trending in our library? Coffee enemas and homemade cat food."

"I had a lady ask where she could find a chastity

belt. Another asked me where she could buy some weed. (I referred them both to the reference desk.)"

"A patron once told me that I couldn't be Mexican because I'm not dark enough. WTF?"

"'You know what would make you a knockout? Lose weight!'"

"'You don't look like a librarian. You should be wearing a shirtwaist dress. With horizontal stripes.'"

"Direct quote from one patron: 'My man shaved *down there*... and I didn't like it one bit. I like a natural man.' What?? (By the way, I work in an elementary school library.)"

"A patron once accused me of running a sex slave ring from the express computers."

"I've been asked to help a patron find a photo of Jesus."

"A woman once asked if I had any hand-me-down clothes I could give her daughter, since we were both 'big girls.'"

"One man, in a misguided attempt to flirt and/or

make me uncomfortable, asked me where we keep the porn. With a straight face, I told him we keep it on the third floor. (It's a two story building.)"

"I was just asked how to make an apple into a bong."

"A patron once told me there was a cat in the ceiling. And, as it turned out, she was right!"

"I can't polish my nails at work anymore because one of our patrons has a fetish and begins giving me sex advice."

"A patron once told me in a stage whisper about her alien abduction, complete with biological details I'd really rather not have heard."

"One patron demanded that my boss fire me for putting a hex on her incarcerated son."

"Somebody just came in to ask if we sell bait for fishing."

"A patron who was grateful for the help I'd given her with a reference question advised me to always store my kitchen knives in the laundry hamper, 'so if someone breaks into your house, they can't use them to stab you.'"

Because librarians are courteous by nature, we can be counted on to respond to your oddball statements, remarks and requests with dignity and grace. My co-worker, for example, patiently endured that little waterpick lecture rather shutting it down with, "What makes you think that my teeth are any of your business?"

Still, the next time you're tempted to share your innermost thoughts about sex, drugs or dental hygiene with your local librarian, do us all a favor.

Think twice.

Don't Call Me Baby!

I've worked at my library long enough to be on a first-name basis with many of our patrons, and the rest greet me with the courtesy and respect that, as a trained professional, I deserve.

Except when they don't. From time to time, a patron will call me "sweetie." Or "honey-bunch." Or "dear." I have to put up with it, but I don't have to like it. And I'm not alone. Recently a fellow librarian posted this lament on Facebook: "A patron just called me baby. Can I go home now?"

The comments this inspired from other librarians were sympathetic:

"I hear you. I've got a Master's Degree in Library Science. So naturally, I want to be greeted with 'Hiya cupcake!'"

"I hate being called pet names. 'Do you have the latest Grisham, lovey?' ICK."

"A patron called me 'doll' the other day. 'This isn't a film noir movie,' I told him. 'And you sure aren't Humphrey Bogart.'"

"I'm not a baby. I'm old enough to collect social security. A little respect, please."

"Today a student half my age called me 'hon.' And an older professor called me 'sweetie.' (Sigh.)"

"Just wait till you're my age. I'm in my sixties and some patrons get a kick out of calling me 'young lady.' They think they're being charming, but it's just a cutesy way of saying 'You're *old*.'"

The clear consensus? Librarians are not babies, kittens or cupcakes.

"I'm constantly being called 'honey' or 'sweetie' -- and I am neither! Grrr."

"We have a patron who calls everyone 'kitten.' We haven't been able to stop him."

"When I go to the hospital, I don't call my doctor 'baby.' Why is it okay to call *me* that?"

"One of my regulars calls me Madam. It always makes me feel like Heidi Fleiss."

"I got called 'honey-baby-sweetie' once. By a woman. I guess she thought it increased her chance of good service. No."

Sometimes, it's just a Southern thing:

"The use of diminutives is particularly Southern. I've come to realize that most of the folks who do it mean no harm. They're just substituting words like 'honey' or 'sweetie' for 'Mr.' or 'Ma'am.'"

"Exactly! When a woman with a southern accent calls me 'hon,' I don't mind."

"I grew up in Virginia and I have a tendency to call people 'sweet pea.' Sometimes I'll slip and call a patron or a co-worker 'sweet pea.' I always apologize."

"I was called 'hon' by a young woman from Georgia not long ago. It was probably a cultural thing, but it was still jarring."

"Agreed. I respond on a case-by-case basis. There are things I let slide with some groups of people that I wouldn't take in stride with others."

"I used to have a great distaste for one patron who always called women 'baby.' But then my son went to work for him and told me that he always calls men the same thing. Ah, the South."

Of course, some patrons can get away with anything:

"We have a patron who calls me 'love,' but he's sixty-five and has a fabulous cockney accent so I don't mind it. He sounds like Michael Caine. But from anyone else? Nope."

"I once had a patron who spoke with the most wonderful drawl. She could tell me to kill and eat my own dogs with that accent and I'd still think she was delightful."

"One of our patrons always calls me 'darlin' but he's an old sweetie so I put up with it."

And a few librarians are actually okay with being kittens:

"Being called 'sweetie' or 'baby' doesn't bother me. I appreciate it when people try to be nice. After all, there are many worse things to be called!"

"Calling people honey-sweetie-dear-lovie isn't

necessarily meant to be demeaning or sexist. And I know from experience that it's a hard habit to break!"

"Everyone has things that offend them. Being called 'sweetie' isn't one for me. As someone who isn't religious, I'm much more bristly when someone tells me to have a 'blessed day.'"

"I have far less tolerance for pet names coming from men than from women. But whether it bothers me usually depends on the tone of the interaction before the pet name was used."

Librarians, by nature, are polite and well-mannered. But sometimes even the nicest librarian will push back:

"Being called 'sweetie' by a patron is a huge pet peeve of mine. I always correct them with 'You can call me by name or Madam Director -- it's up to you.'"

"I had a patron who always called me 'baby.' I just ignored him until he finally changed to 'Ma'am.'"

We have a patron who calls everyone 'cupcake' and I always respond, 'That's *Doctor* Cupcake to you, pal.' (I'm a doctor of jurisprudence.)"

My favorite solution?

"I always respond to people who call me diminutives that make me feel uncomfortable by calling them 'Hoss' and giving them a hard stare. It works really well."

I can't wait to try that.

If every time a librarian were called 'baby,' they could take the rest of the day off, maybe that would stop the practice. Even better? Every time you call me "sweetie" or "baby," I get to place a small "annoying patron fine" on your account.

If that doesn't change your behavior, at least my putting up with your lack of respect would benefit my library.

In the meantime, sugar, here's a little advice. If you want me to waive your overdue fine? Don't call me "baby."

It's A Taxing Time To Be A Librarian

The fifteenth of April is on the horizon, and librarians all over the country are bracing themselves for the sea of patrons who are about to surge, tsunami-like, into our workplaces, demanding tax forms.

Over the next few months I'll get to replay, countless times, one of my favorite little exchanges:

Library Patron: Where are the tax forms?

Me: Right under that GIGANTIC SIGN that says TAX FORMS.

Libraries exist to serve the public and we librarians enjoy being helpful. And at tax time, we can be. Provided, of course, that the IRS has sent us all of the forms and instructional booklets that our patrons need.

And that's the challenge. More often than not, they haven't. We get the booklets without the forms. Or the forms without the booklets. Or we get everything our patrons need, but not enough of it.

Sometimes, we get nothing at all.

There's no apparent rhyme or reason to what material each library receives. Sometimes, though, everything works out perfectly. Yesterday, a librarian posted on Facebook that her library had just received a full set of tax forms and instruction booklets.

Her fellow librarians responded with:

"You actually got *booklets*? I'm so jealous."

"We got our forms yesterday. But no instruction books. Wah."

"So far we have five boxes of instructional booklets for the 1040A. And NOTHING ELSE."

"We were a little freaked out yesterday when we got ten consecutive e-mails from the IRS telling us our 1040EZ booklets had shipped. One at a time, apparently."

"We didn't get any forms at all! We have to refer everyone to the internet."

"No lovin' from the IRS so far for our little library. They must not want our patrons' money."

Many libraries will never receive every form and booklet the public needs, resulting in countless frustrated library patrons, some of whom will take their tax-time rage and anxiety out on us. They'll call us rude names. They'll insist that the forms they want are in the library somewhere and demand that we search harder for them.

A few will even accuse us of hiding the forms from them out of spite.

Some librarians, in response, take far too much pleasure in telling disagreeable patrons that we haven't got the form they came in for.

"We ran out of tax forms yesterday," one librarian recently commented on Facebook, "and I have to admit that by April, I actually enjoy telling certain folks that we're all out. Of course, by tomorrow, we may get them all in again."

"Don't worry," responded another. "If your library is anything like mine, you'll run out again within a week and you can enjoy letting people down again."

Yes, we can help you go online and print out anything you need. But you'd be surprised at how many people are horrified and affronted to learn that they'll have to cough up fifteen cents per page to make this happen.

A free tax form, they seem to believe, is their God-given right as library patrons and United States citizens.

I have, on more than one occasion, paid to print out a patron's tax forms myself just to get rid of them (while intoning this silent incantation over each form as it emerged from the printer: "Audit me! Audit me!")

I know that you really don't want your favorite librarian to long to see you audited. So on behalf of librarians everywhere I'd just like to say: Please calm down. We can get through this. Don't scream at us. We're trying to help you.

On the morning of April fifteenth, as we prepare to open the library, we can count on the fact that there will be at least one person waiting at the door, begging us to let them in early so they can grab one final form.

And on April sixteenth? We'll take down the gigantic TAX FORMS sign, put it back in the storage closet and relax. Until next year.

The Library Witch

Kathryn wanders through the library hugging herself and muttering. In her seventies, with scraggly grey hair and a hard, troubled gaze, she resembles a witch, but in baggy sweats and a faded T-shirt instead of a black dress and pointy hat. Because Kathryn once taught nursery school and is drawn to small children, she'll hover by the elevator to the junior room. When the kids get off, she'll be standing there, towering over them and glowering. When they shriek with fear, she's as alarmed as they are.

Kathyrn also alarms our adult patrons, but since she doesn't technically interfere with their use of the library, there's nothing library staff can do. Being weird and inappropriate, while troubling, doesn't violate any specific library rule of behavior.

Kathryn chants nonsense in a singsong voice and emits bleats and clicking sounds, but quietly. The fact that she'll sometimes slip a hand down her pants and scratch her butt is a little icky, but not illegal. She's in a grey area both cognitively and in terms of library policy. She doesn't really belong here but we can't kick her out.

But some of us would like to.

We're a small library and having Kathryn here for hours each day has made a difference. Before Kathryn, we were a pleasant, bustling library. Now we're a bustling, creepy library -- the library with the wandering witch.

Joe, the man who brings Kathryn in, isn't her husband. We don't know what he is. All we know is that he sits down at a computer and leaves her to wander the library unsupervised. But she isn't really unsupervised. He knows that library staff will stop her from invading the staff room, playing with the water fountain or wandering out the front door.

"It takes a village to look after your demented girlfriend while you go online and pretend that she doesn't exist," one co-worker muttered angrily after an afternoon devoted to keeping Kathryn out of harm's way.

"Cut the guy some slack," said another. "I'm happy to give him a break. Would you want to be in his shoes?"

She may not be his girlfriend. Maybe she was, once. Joe isn't loving or affectionate with her. Nor is he angry or testy. Mostly, he's exasperated.

"Sit down, Kathryn!" he'll instruct sternly when we bring her back to him. "Stay with me."

A moment later, he returns to web surfing and she's off again.

A friend of mine who lives on their block tells me that their once tidy home is run down and packed with junk. When Kathryn gets out and wanders the neighborhood, near-naked and shouting, the cops just return her to Joe.

"Can't you do something?" my friend has asked them.

They told her that removing Kathryn from her home and institutionalizing her wouldn't necessarily make her life any better. "That's what will happen if you call social services," they said. "Are you sure you want to make that call?"

She wasn't. Neither am I.

Perhaps there is some tenderness there. Maybe the two of them bed down together at night, and she's glad to have him. He seems to be all she has left. The loving constellation of family and friends we count on to take care of us has let her down.

We librarians, all of us strong, independent middle-aged women, tell ourselves this won't happen to us.

The public library is the heart of any community. Young parents bring in their newborns -- tiny, loved and full of promise. Couples in their eighties come in, holding hands. When you work at a public library you see every kind of person, at every stage of life. You see where you've been and where you're going. You see both the future you want and the future you dread.

What will become of Kathryn? She'll probably continue to haunt our library until she manages to spark a conflict with one of our more volatile patrons, perhaps the skinny bald paranoid who hisses at you if she thinks you're looking at her funny. Kathryn will glance at Old Baldy the wrong way and the next thing you know we'll have a cat fight on our hands. Then we'll call in the cops and have them both banned from the building.

It will be a relief to have our pleasant library back. But we'll feel as if we've let Kathryn down. Of course, she doesn't belong here. Maybe the real problem is that she doesn't belong anywhere.

Are You A Mystery? Or A Trashy Romance?

A librarian recently posted an intriguing question on Facebook: If you were being sold in a library book sale, which table would you be on?"

She had her first response within seconds:

"Damaged."

Quickly followed by:

"Mystery!"

"Adventure."

"Bible stories. (I'm born again.)"

"True crime. (I work in a prison library.)"

"Humor books, of course. (They're easy to read and

you walk away smiling.)"

As more librarians got into the game, the comments poured in:

"Withdrawn."

"Inspirational. (I want to make a difference in the lives of others.)"

"Overlooked gems."

"Audiobooks. (I never shut up.)"

A few responses were both insightful and descriptive:

"I'm the book leveling out the table the other books are arranged on."

"I'd be under the table, out of sight and forgotten, in a waterlogged box full of baby spiders."

But most of the comments were limited to a few quick words:

"Oddities."

"Fantasy!"

"Trivia."

"Self-help."

"I'm a trashy romance!"

Some answers would seem to reflect low self-esteem:

"Hurt."

"Distressed."

"Never checked out."

"Fragile. Handle with care."

Others, not so much:

"Rare finds."

"Classics."

"One-of-a-kind."

"Valuable."

A few comments referenced the fact that some of us are getting on in years:

"Old and unusual."

"Used but useful."

"Cover shows wear but contents still good."

"Vintage and fabulous."

And then there were the librarians who walk on the wild side:

"Banned books."

"Dangerous! Adults only!"

"Forbidden... but alluring."

"Sexy!"

"Cheap and easy (snicker)."

My very favorite response? (And entirely realistic, given this crowd?):

"Scratched by cats."

In conclusion? One of the many joys of library work is having such clever, fun-loving colleagues. As far as I'm concerned? We're all Rare Finds.

Leaping Librarian!

For my last annual check-up, I had a bone density scan and got a nasty surprise.

Like far too many women my age, I've got osteoporosis.

"But I walk for at least an hour a day!" I protested to my doctor. "And I'm always carrying books around at the library where I work. Isn't checking in a gigantic tome like *The Goldfinch* just like weight-lifting?"

Apparently not.

She told me that although all that walking is great for my health and keeps me lean, I am -- ironically -- too lean for it to constitute the kind of weight-bearing exercise that would strengthen my skeleton.

(Here's the bright side for those of you who are struggling to lose those last ten pounds. Don't! Carrying that extra weight around is good for your bones.)

I've also got several bad habits that, over the years, have leached the calcium out of my bones -- drinking lots of coffee and over-salting my food.

My doc has given me a year to do what I can to strengthen my bones. Or else? I'll have to start taking those meds that Sally Fields is always pushing on TV.

I've researched what I can do to improve my bone density.

The answer?

Prunes!

One study concluded that when postmenopausal women ate six prunes a day, it improved their bone density.

Another thing I can do?

Jumping!

Women who jump twenty times a day, according to a different study, also improve their bone density.

From now on, just think of me as the prune-eating, leaping librarian.

(Prunes being what they are, I'm lucky that my digestive system is so sturdy, or I'd be the leaping farting librarian.)

I now keep a supply of prunes in the staff fridge. The upside? Unlike my former go-to snack, vanilla jelly beans, my new snack supply lasts a lot longer, since none of my co-workers ever ask if they can have one.

The downside? They're prunes.

Now, when you approach the circulation desk at the library where I work, I'll leap into the air before asking "How can I help you?"

How have our patrons responded to this behavior? So far, they've been too polite and well-mannered to mention it, with the exception of the one dude who grinned and asked if I was working on my David Lee Roth imitation.

I've also stopped over-salting my food. And I've cut

down (a little) on my coffee drinking. It's too early to tell if any of this is doing me any good. Check back in a year. In the meantime? If you haven't gotten a bone density scan, I encourage you to do so.

The sooner you get on it, the better for your bones.

I do hope that your bones, unlike mine, are fabulous. But, the next time you come into my library, if I leap into the air before asking "How may I help you?" and you leap into the air before asking if I can put *Strong Women, Strong Bones* on hold for you, I'll leap into the air again and say "Certainly."

Then I'll offer you a prune.

Putting The Cuss In Customer Service

After graciously coping with a library patron who began yelling at me when I told him that he had to pay the whopping fine on his card before he could check out any more DVDs, I logged onto Facebook and asked my fellow librarians: "Have you ever been tempted to swear at work? And have you ever given in to this temptation?"

Within a day, I'd received eighty-four responses. A sampling?

"Fuck yeah, I curse at work! But never in front of patrons."

"If a patron is near, I limit myself to 'son of a monkey!'"

"Are you kidding me? I put the 'cuss' in 'customer

service.'"

"I shout '*Kuken*,' the Swedish word for 'dick,' whenever I drop something."

"Alas, we aren't allowed to swear at my library, so I have to fall back on 'fudge' or 'darn.'"

"I actually told my boss when I interviewed for this job that swearing was one of my flaws. And I got the job!"

"I swore at work today, while using a computer. That's why they call it a 'cursor.'"

"I can swear in four languages, which just came in handy when I dropped a volume of the OED on my foot while working in the library of a Southern Baptist college and cut loose with a fluid stream of invective... in French."

"I consider swearing to be the last refuge of the inarticulate. That being said, if you don't swear much, when you do swear it surprises the shit out of people."

"My husband likes to use words that sound like swear words but aren't. His current favorite? 'G. Gordon Liddy!'"

"Working in the Children's Room means that I have to employ alternatives. I use 'Drat' and 'What the deuce!' Frequently."

I work at a high school library. I always substitute the word 'plum' for the F-bomb. As in 'Caleb, what the plum are you wearing?'"

"One of my co-workers shouts 'Bad word! Bad word! Bad word!'"

"This week after I swore in front of one of our sweet young teen pages, I apologized and she laughed at me."

"I swear all the time. But I'm a sailor and it's an important part of our culture, so don't try to oppress me."

"Strong emotions call for strong language. And we librarians are passionate people, right? We sure as fuck aren't in this for the money."

"If I couldn't curse at work I would fucking explode!"

In conclusion? Shut up and pay your fine without giving us any guff, you son of a monkey. Unless you want to see your librarian explode.

A Quiet Revolution

In the many years I've worked at my suburban library, I've noticed that people have a tendency to take care of their own. I'm not saying that librarians are unfair. But each of us has a certain amount of discretion and I've noticed some patterns in how we make use of it.

For instance? I'm Jewish. If a library patron is Jewish, we begin any transaction with a certain level of trust. If you owe a fine, I won't let you off the hook just because we share the same faith. But if you give me a good excuse? I'm likely to believe you.

I once had a co-worker who was politically conservative and strongly pro-life. If you came into the library wearing a pro-choice button, she'd treat you with civility. But she wasn't going to do you any favors.

On the other hand, if you gave her a plausible reason for keeping that copy of *If Democrats Had Any Brains, They'd Be Republicans* past the due date, your fine just might get waived.

A while back, after noticing that one white co-worker consistently gave white patrons the benefit of the doubt, but was more by-the-book with patrons of color, I took a hard look at my own behavior. Did I share her bias? I didn't think so, but, just to be sure, I resolved, from then on, to go out of my way to adopt an even-handed "customer is always right" approach.

If you give me an excuse for bringing a DVD back late, or swear that the dog training book you've just returned had those bite marks on the cover when you checked it out, I'll trust that you're telling me the truth, unless I have good reason to doubt you.

Does this cost the library money? Perhaps. But I hope that what we lose in fines, we gain in public trust. It's important that all our patrons feel that they're being treated fairly.

I was recently tempted to take it a step further.

I'd just read an illuminating essay by Ta-Nehisi Coates, who convincingly demonstrates that African Americans continue to suffer the devastating impact of 250 years of slavery, 90 years of Jim Crow, 60 years of separate-but-equal, and 35 years of racist housing policy. The United States Government, Coates concludes, should pay reparations to the descendants of African-American slaves in order to help undo this enduring legacy of racism.

I totally agree with him. But I don't think that's ever going to happen.

A few days after I read that essay, an African American patron returned three overdue DVDs, which resulted in a large fine. She asked, as patrons often do, if I'd consider cutting her a break.

And which point this word floated into my head: *reparations*.

There was little I could do to end the impact of 250 years of racism on African Americans in this country. But I could make things a little easier for this particular African American library patron.

So I did.

Did I tell her that I'd waived her fine because, as someone who'd enjoyed white privilege every day of my life, Coates had inspired me to do something, however small, to push back against the systemic racism she copes with on a daily basis?

Of course not. She would have thought I was a lunatic.

Can my action be justified as a form of ad hoc, from-the-ground-up reparations? If every white person who read Coates starting doing this kind of thing, would it help level the playing field? Or was this a totally misguided exercise of reverse racism that deprived my library of badly needed funds? I don't know. You tell me.

Clearly, it's not my library's job to fix racism. Nor was my action a well-thought out solution to a serious problem. It was just an impulsive gesture. I don't know if Coates would applaud that impulse or call me a fool. But we librarians waive fines every day, for a variety of reasons. We're allowed to use our discretion. I decided that day to use mine.

I might just do it again.

Library Lost and Found

From time to time a patron will check a book or DVD out of the library where I work and then misplace it. After we extend the due date to give them a little extra time to search, they'll usually find the missing item under a car seat or behind a book shelf. But library material can turn up in surprising places. After a patron returned a long overdue DVD that she'd found, while spring cleaning, underneath her microwave, I asked my fellow librarians: "What's the oddest place that a patron has ever found a misplaced library book or DVD?"

As a public service, I've decided to share some of their responses with the library-going public:

"A patron just found an overdue CD under the spare tire in her trunk."

"I once paid for a lost picture book, then found it years later when we moved the bookshelf in my son's room to paint the walls."

"One of our patrons just found a long overdue book in his dachshund's toy box."

"Just got a letter from a patron telling us that she'd found a lost copy of *Finding Dory* in a potted plant."

"I once found an overdue library book hidden under my grandson's mattress. He confessed that he loved the book and didn't want to give it up."

"As a parent who often hides DVDs from her toddler, I can attest to the fact that 'under the microwave' is not a weird place to find, say, *Thomas The Tank Engine.*"

"When we replaced our refrigerator, we found a children's book that the cat had apparently batted underneath it to join her stash of rubber bands and milk jar rings."

"Mom: I thought we already returned that.
Kid: No, it's in the Barbie house."

"I once discovered an overdue paperback inside a recliner."

"I have a friend who puts library books in her deep freeze 'to kill the bedbugs' and has been known to forget them there."

"A patron was having some work done on her house. When they opened up one of the walls, they found a stack of picture books that had been accidentally dry-walled over during a previous renovation."

"On top of a ceiling fan blade! The patron, a college student, thinks a friend must have hidden it there as a joke. He found it months later when he turned on the fan and the book went flying."

"Several patrons have returned library DVDs they found at yard sales or in pawn shops."

"One patron swore up and down that she'd returned a whole slew of books, only to find them the following fall when she unpacked her Christmas decorations."

"A patron once found an overdue DVD under her stove. Her kids were playing 'DVD soccer' in the kitchen and kicked it under there."

"We had a patron who swore the DVD he'd borrowed had vanished into thin air. Turned out that he'd left it on the roof of his truck, then drove off. Another patron found it in a ditch and brought it in."

"A patron once brought back a book that she found in her washing machine. It had been thrown in with a load of sheets and went through the entire wash cycle. (And yes, it was beyond repair and she had to pay for it.)"

"A mom once found an overdue board book in her wok. Her toddler left it there while playing in the cupboard."

"Because patrons often find overdue books under the car seat, we always recommend that people check there. One patron protested that he didn't have a car -- but he later found the missing book under the car seat of the guy who sells him pot!"

The next time you lose a library book, be sure to check the usual places. Under your car seat. In the trunk. Behind the bookshelf. Then try inside the freezer and the washing machine, and on top of all the ceiling fans.

And don't forget to check under the microwave.

Librarians! Here's A Little Snark to Brighten Your Day

Although some members of the public imagine that librarians are paid to sit around on our *tushies* reading all day, anyone who actually works at a library knows that it's a tough, challenging job. Library work can be stressful. But laughter is a great way to relieve stress, which is why I follow @LousyLibrarian on Twitter.

Every day, @LousyLibrarian posts a snarky, insightful and often hilarious Tweet about library life. So who is @LousyLibrarian? When I reached out, I learned that they wish to remain anonymous, disclosing no information about age, gender or location of library workplace.

All I know is that @LousyLibrarian a sanity-saver

if you're reeling from an encounter with a toxic patron or just feeling overwhelmed by your workload. Here are a few of my favorite Tweets:

The only things librarians love as much as cats are space heaters.

"Why are these shelves labeled 'Holiday Books?'"

"Because 'Substandard Obligatory Seasonal Cash-Grabs' would've worn out the label maker."

"My library card isn't working."

"I'm not an expert but I think that might be because it's a hotel room key card."

"I requested a book this morning. Is it there yet?"

"Depends. Did you click the 'Defy All Laws of Time and Space' box?"

Am promoting the new Grisham to hipsters as an artisanal melange of hand-crafted lawyer book clichés.

Patron: "Someone here was unpleasant to me five years ago."

Me: "Wow, that's impressive; you're like a grudge archivist."

Patron just asked if he could change clothes in the restroom. Hoping he's Clark Kent.

Once I weeded a Patterson in Reno just to watch it die.

"We've got a problem with a patron."

"Which patron?"

"The weird guy with the weird pants."

"You're gonna have to be more specific."

This patron interaction has been brought to you by the letters T, M and I.

"This computer keeps saying my email password's wrong. Can I move to another one?"

"You might try going to a computer in another area code."

We have an informally designated napping area in the library. It's called the library.

It's nice to be around people who approach books with enthusiasm and curiosity. But today I have to go to our Library Book Club instead.

"Is it too late for me to register to vote?"

"Not if you're voting for Librarian With The Most Disappointing News."

It is apparently a rule that when you ask me how to print stuff out you must first detail the woes that have befallen your home printer.

"What do you do with magazines when you withdraw them?"

"We thank them for their sacrifice and shred them before an image of Helen Gurley Brown."

I enjoy our weekly chats about whether Lisa Gardner has a new book out yet. The same way Sisyphus enjoyed his little hikes.

The word "Webinar" comes from the Greek for "You're not going to learn anything."

For my Halloween costume I should have dressed as a stolen Blu-ray; then I could just not be here despite what all the records say.

"I've read all of Nichols Spark's books. What would you recommend?"

"Ritual suicide?"

"Do you have any recommendations for someone who just doesn't like books?"

"How about this nice stapler?"

"I need to pay bills online and I've never touched anything electronic before. Can you help?"

"I'm sorry. I don't think I work here anymore."

I don't know who @LousyLibrarian is, but I'm a library humorist myself, and when I finally get my library sitcom up and running, @LousyLibrarian will be the first person I hire for my writers' room.

Until that happens, I'll continue to enjoy their posts on Twitter.

I'll Read What She's Reading

A French start-up is marketing a Bluetooth-enabled vibrator that's paired with an erotic Ebook. During the smutty parts, you just tap the screen or shake the device and the vibrator starts right up.

"It's going to generate some buzz," quipped gadget reviewer Nate Hoffelder.

A librarian pal just posted a description of this new product on Facebook, asking, "Who volunteers to be the first librarian to add these to their collection?"

The first response?

"There's not enough bleach in the world."

The comments that followed were just as dismissive:

"My prediction? It will come and go."

"This puts a brand new spin on Book Club."

"I can't wait for the first patron who brings one in and asks me to help set it up."

"I wouldn't look forward to checking it back in. But honestly? It would probably have fewer germs on it than the average board book."

Here's what I think. The folks who dreamed up this device are missing an important opportunity. What a terrific way to motivate reluctant readers! Nobody needs an incentive to read erotica. But if I'd known that I'd be rewarded with an orgasm at the end of every chapter, I might have actually opened my high school chemistry textbook.

Why not pair a vibrator with each copy of the tax code? Or *Medicare for Dummies*?

What if we could special order Vibrating Bestsellers to get us through those ultra-boring Book Group reads? We could turn *The Goldfinch* from a big yawn into a big yippee.

And what about Vibrating Classics? Maybe I'll finally be able to finish *Middlemarch*!

Literature, in the twenty-first century, may be struggling. But vibrating literature? It's just getting started.

Even so, if you're expecting to be able to check one of these "books with extra buzz" out of your local library? I have the feeling it's going to be a very long wait.

How Quiet Does A Library Have To Be?

The library where I work just received an irate letter from a patron who complained that my workplace was too noisy, citing crying babies, ill-behaved children and library staff talking too loudly with patrons and with each other. Because I've always thought of us as happily bustling rather than raucous, I logged onto Facebook, where I shared my story, then asked my fellow librarians, "Do you work in a quiet library? How quiet should a public library be?"

Response was swift:

"It's 2017! Libraries aren't shush-factories anymore."

"Silent libraries are a thing of the past."

"Libraries reflect their communities, and mine is full of young families. Quiet? No!"

"Tell him to put on headphones."

"We gave up the quiet rule in 1996 and never looked back. We love our busy, crowded library."

Within a day, seventy-five librarians had weighed in. The consensus? Libraries are no longer silent. Nor should they be! Here's a sampling of what my peers had to say:

How Quiet Does A Library Have To Be?

"Libraries have evolved. These days they're culture and community centers where people can gather, enjoy programs and get information. Patrons who expect absolute quiet need to adjust."

"We've hosted drumming circles, line dancers and mariache programs! #notquiet."

"When Story Times are in progress or the quilters are meeting (which means lots of laughter and chatter) we're anything but silent. A bustling library is a well-loved library."

"We think it's great that a lot of kids come here to

just hang out. When I receive noise complaints, I explain that libraries are for using. Embrace your loud library!"

"We recently had a patron suggest that we close all the crying babies up in a room. Hello? Libraries don't have to be silent. Fight that antiquated crap with all your energy!"

"We're a branch library in a busy neighborhood. You should hear us during a packed Family Story time or on Harry Potter night. I love the hum of a happy library."

"After a group of senators used our meeting room, one told me, 'This has got to be the loudest library I've ever been in!' How did I respond? I said 'Thank you.'"

A Library Can Be Too Quiet.

"I visited another branch yesterday and it was silent as the grave. Kinda creeped me out. I definitely prefer a library with some chatter."

"A too-silent library is unwelcoming."

"I worked in a totally quiet library once. It was quiet because nobody ever used it! It had refused to change to meet modern needs and had become obsolete."

Quiet Space Is A Must.

"A quiet place to read, work or study is a core service libraries should provide. Does that mean the entire library must be silent? Of course not!"

"We aren't a quiet library, but we do have a quiet reading room."

"Our silent reading room doesn't get much use, but it's important to have it for those folks who prefer quiet to the bustle of our community-oriented main floor."

"Because we can't afford a silent reading room, we provide disposable earplugs to any patron who asks."

You Can Find Quiet If You're Willing To Be Flexible.

"My library gets crazy busy and loud but there are times we're not as busy and patrons who require quiet have learned to visit us then."

"I was thrilled yesterday when a patron who'd been complaining about volume brought in noise-cancelling headphones."

Today's Librarian Is Reluctant To Shush.

"When an older patron complains about noise, we explain that libraries have changed, then find them a seat away from the fray."

"During Story Time, I encourage the children to shout and roar and bark and meow. They bring energy and life to the library!"

It's A Public Library, Not A Cocktail Party.

"My branch recently got a noise complaint via Twitter about the staff talking too loud. Welcome to the modern world!"

"Staff conversation is an issue for us too. It's great that we enjoy each other's company. Not-so-great is the fact that we sometimes forget the patrons can hear us yakking."

"For some of our older patrons, especially those who live alone, conversation with library staff is a high point of their visit. The last thing we want to do is shut that down!"

And Finally, My Favorite Comment?

"If library noise volume is an issue, maybe we need a Dewey Decibel System!"

When I applied to work at the Bala Cynwyd Library, I was told that it wasn't a quiet place. "If you need a silent workplace," the library's director said to me, "you're applying for the wrong job." Eighteen years later, I'm still here and I love my bustling library. The way I see it, a library is the heart of any community. And you wouldn't want your heart to fall silent, would you?

That being said, in the future, when I sing our praises to the rooftops, I'll try to keep my voice down.

How To Make A Librarian Happy

I love my library job, but sometimes our patrons make it tougher than it needs to be. I recently asked my fellow librarians to help me create a "wish list" of things, big and small, serious and frivolous, that you can do to make your favorite librarian happy.

So what can you do, as a member of the library-going public, to help us better serve our patrons and enjoy our jobs?

1. Greet me before launching into your request. You don't have to ask how I am. Just say "Hello."

2. Your library card? Don't leave home without it.

3. Return everything on time, or pay your fines

with a smile.

4. Please keep the phone calls, food and drama outside.

5. Push in your chair after you use the computer.

6. Don't come to the library if you have a contagious illness. We love our patrons, but not their colds.

7. Put away your phone when you're talking to me.

8. Don't toss your trash in the book drop.

9. Say "please" and "thank-you."

10. Keep in mind that librarians are only human. When we make mistakes, don't scream at us. Instead, try to be forgiving.

11. Moms and nannies? Stop gabbing with each other during Story Time. Enjoy the songs, stories and rhymes with your children.

12. Learn to use the catalog computer.

13. Wait your turn instead of interrupting when I'm helping somebody else.

14. Please don't look at porn on our computers.

15. Don't snap your fingers to get my attention. I'm not a dog.

16. Let us know how the babies and toddlers we sang to at Story Time are doing now that they've grown. We love to hear about them.

17. Never apologize for bothering me with a reference question. It's not a bother. It's my job.

18. Don't go ballistic when we won't let you check material out without your library card or identification.

19. Supervise your kids. Don't let them run wild. This is a library, not a playground.

20. This isn't Match.com. Stop hitting on library staff.

21. Don't slip the book Fido chewed up into the book drop and hope we don't notice the damage. Fess up. Say "My Labradoodle ruined this book and I'd like to pay for it."

22. Please refrain from discussing your religious

or political beliefs with me.

23. Ask with a fully formed question. Don't just walk up to the reference desk and blurt out "London" or "Aztecs."

24. Don't *ever* call me "girl."

25. Bathe. And for the love of Pete, please brush your teeth before leaning in to ask me a reference question.

26. Don't ask me to show you how to use the photocopier when what you really want is for me to do your photocopying for you.

27. Please please please don't attempt to re-shelve the books! That's our job and we're happy to do it.

28. Don't wear so much perfume. I can't assist you if I can't breathe.

29. Don't use risqué photos, strips of bacon, cigarette butts or unused condoms as bookmarks.

30. Communicate with me using words, not grunts or blank stares.

31. Don't cough all over your library card and then hand it to me.

32. Don't come into the library unless you're at least kind of sober.

33. Before you glare at me for talking too loudly to a patron, consider that the patron I'm talking to might be hard of hearing.

34. Clean up after yourself when you leave. Don't make us pick up your dirty tissues, candy wrappers and coffee cups.

35. Don't expect me to bend the rules for you (or curse at me when I won't).

36. Don't try to apply for a new library card two minutes before we close.

37. Don't steal our DVDs.

38. Leave promptly at closing time. Don't make us wait around while you finish your last minute photocopying.

39. Be kind to both library staff and library materials.

40. Write the library a check during our fund drive, advocate for library funding, tell everyone how much you love the library and come back often. We wouldn't be here without you.

And if you take the trouble to bake us a batch of cookies, send us a holiday card or write us a thank you note? It will make our day.

Turn the page to read an excerpt from Roz's next book, *My Relationship Tanked And All I Got Was This Best-Selling Memoir.*

Not Sure If You're Actually Having Sex? I Can Help.

When I stumbled upon evidence that the man I'd loved and trusted for twenty years had a secret girlfriend for the past ten of those years, he tried to deny it.

"We never had sex!" he told me. And I believed him. For about two minutes.

"You never kissed?"

"We did kiss."

"Did you hug and grope?"

"We did."

"Did you take your clothes off?"

"Yes."

"Did you give each other orgasms?"

"Yes. But -- we never fucked!"

If he's to be believed (and maybe he's not, since he's clearly an accomplished liar) they had a secret love affair going for 10 years but they never once had good old-fashioned sexual intercourse.

I'll admit that once Mike confessed that he and Maggie had done everything else, part of me thought, "If you've gone that far, why stop? For goodness sakes, you're already committing adultery. Why not go ahead and bonk?"

Deniability.

"This isn't really sex!" they assured each other, and Mike, later, told me. "So what we're doing isn't wrong."

Apparently, this is how a cheater thinks. They flirted and phone-sexed and kissed and emailed and said "I love you" and made passionate furtive whoopee in hotel rooms, but they convinced themselves that it wasn't cheating because "we didn't have sex."

Translation: We did everything two lovers can do. Except *schtup*.

And this isn't sex??

On what planet?

When my friends learned about Mike and Maggie, many more than I'd have thought confided that their boyfriends, husbands and/or dads had played by the same rules. They had affairs that they justified as not really being affairs because there was no intercourse.

Hell, even the President of the United States was on board. "I did not have sexual relations with that woman!"

Yeah. Except for all the blow jobs.

There's a reason they call it oral sex and not oral philosophy or oral sunshine, rainbows and moonbeams.

Clearly, we've got a linguistic problem here.

So? In the interest of better communication, I'd like to get a few definitions on the table. If the two of you get a hotel room together? You're guilty. Even if you don't enjoy penetration. Even if all of your clothes don't come off. Even if you only roll around and smooch and tell each other what special little snowflakes you are.

Even if the two of you are just sitting there together, fully clothed, reading the Bible.

You're still having sex and you know it.

I'm calling that out. That's sex. In fact, going forward, I'm calling it Mike-and-Maggie.

If you and another person are doing things that you know your partner wouldn't be okay with?

That's sex!

What kind of sex is it?

It's M&M.

All I know is that I'm never falling for a guy who's into M&M again.

Our Bodies, Our Shelves: A Collection of Library Humor

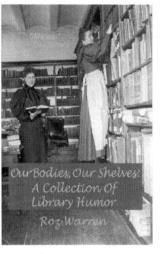

There are eight million stories at your local public library -- and not all of them are in the books! Join humorist Roz Warren for a fascinating behind-the-scenes look at library life. What really goes on behind the circulation desk? And in the stacks? Roz, who writes for everyone from The New York Times to The Funny Times, tells all! What's the strangest bookmark ever left in a library book? What's the lamest excuse ever given for not returning a DVD on time? And what does your favorite librarian *really* think about you? In twenty entertaining essays, you'll meet librarians fighting crime, partying with porn stars, coping with impossible patrons, locating hard-to-find books and saving the world. The most closely-guarded library secrets will be revealed. You'll never look at your local public library the same away again!

HumorOutcasts Press
$14.99
ISBN 0-692-406468
EAN-13 978-069240646-5

Book Roz To Speak At Your Next Event

Library Humorist Roz Warren provides a fascinating behind-the-scenes look at library life with a crowd-pleasing presentation based upon her books *Our Bodies, Our Shelves* and *Just Another Day At Your Local Public Library.*

Roz, who writes for everyone from *The Funny Times* to *The New York Times* (and has appeared on both *Morning Edition* and *The Today Show*) will delight and entertain your audience with surprising tales about life behind the circulation desk. Roz has spoken at churches, synagogues, book groups, museums and libraries, and would love to speak to your group.

"Roz is very warm and welcoming and very approachable. She has a wonderful sense of humor and is a great speaker. We so enjoyed her sharing her stories about library work. Laughter is important and Roz has a great way of making people laugh."
- Ellen Matzner, President, Temple Brith Achim Sisterhood

"Roz Warren put on one of the most delightful programs I can remember, and the audience, one of the largest we've ever gotten, was utterly charmed."
-- Janet Michaelson, Speakers Series Chair for the Bala Cynwyd Library

If you would like Roz Warren to speak at your event, please contact:
Donna Cavanagh
HumorOutcasts Press   Phone: 484-686-2756
Donna@HOPress-ShorehouseBooks.com

About the Author

Roz Warren works at the circulation desk of the Bala Cynwyd Library in suburban Philadelphia. She also writes, often about library work, for *The New York Times*, *The Funny Times*, *The Philadelphia Inquirer*, *The Christian Science Monitor*, *The Jewish Forward*, *Reader's Digest*, *Purple Clover*, *Zestnow*, and *The Huffington Post*.

Roz has appeared on both *The Today Show* and *Morning Edition*.

She's the author of *Our Bodies, Our Shelves: A Collection of Library Humor* and the editor of the ground-breaking Women's Glib women's humor collections, including titles like *The Best Contemporary Women's Humor*, *Men Are From Detroit, Women Are From Paris* and *When Cats Talk Back*.

Roz is also the curator of the "Library Laughs" Facebook page.

Just Another Day At Your Local Public Library is her fourteenth humor book.

You can read more of Roz Warren's work on her website, www.rosalindwarren.com, connect with her on Facebook at www.facebook.com/writerrozwarren, email her at roswarren@gmail.com or follow her on Twitter at @WriterRozWarren.

48276844R00093

Made in the USA
San Bernardino, CA
21 April 2017